Fairy Unicorns

Kingdom Under the Sea

Zanna Davidson

Illustrated by

Nuno Alexandre Vieira

Meet the Unicorns

Tio
Sea Queen
Eirra
Shadow

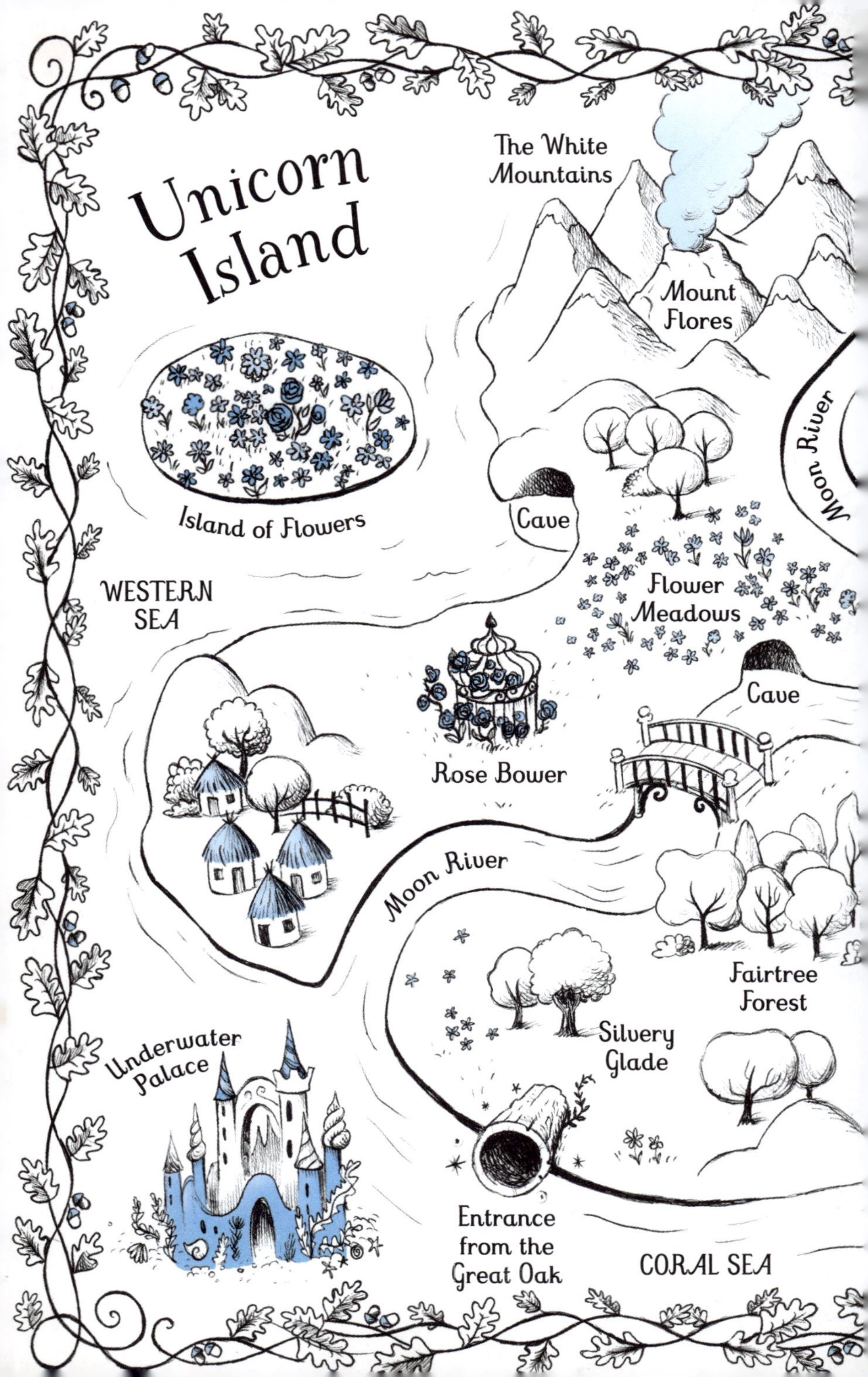
Unicorn Island
The White Mountains
Mount Flores
Moon River
Island of Flowers
Cave
Flower Meadows
WESTERN SEA
Cave
Rose Bower
Moon River
Fairtree Forest
Silvery Glade
Underwater Palace
Entrance from the Great Oak
CORAL SEA

NORTHERN SEA
Towering Cliffs
Jewelled Tree
Cloud Castle
Unicorn King's Castle
Lyra Tree
Ragged Cliffs
EASTERN SEA
Sparkling Lake
Unicorn Valley
N
W
E
S

Contents

Chapter One 7

Chapter Two 19

Chapter Three 31

Chapter Four 50

Chapter Five 61

Chapter Six 80

Chapter Seven 93

Chapter One

Zoe listened to the clock chiming midnight, her excitement rising with each stroke. Then she crept out of bed, her heart beating fast. She was staying with her Great Aunt May for the spring holidays – the first time since Christmas. It had been four whole months since she'd visited Unicorn Island, the secret world hidden inside the great oak tree. And now, she couldn't wait to go back.

From the gentle snores coming down the corridor, Zoe guessed that Great Aunt May was fast asleep at last. Opening the cupboard beside her bed, she took out a cage, woven from vines. Inside, was Shadow, her fairy pony. She placed the cage on the windowsill, so Shadow could see the moonlight and bathe in the fresh spring air. But she didn't unlock the cage... It was bound by magic, and even if it hadn't been, she wouldn't have dared. Shadow might be tiny, small enough to fit into the palm of her hand, and he might look powerless, even sweet – but Zoe knew better. In the past, he had caused chaos, plotting to take over Unicorn Island.

Zoe took one last look at Shadow, and

tiptoed towards the door.

"Do you promise you'll take my message to the Unicorn King?" whispered Shadow.

"I promise," Zoe replied, holding up the little note he had given her.

She slipped it into her bag and tiptoed down the stairs, out through the back door, and into the silvery moonlight.

At the end of the garden path stood the Great Oak, its branches silhouetted against the night sky. Zoe reached into her bag and pulled out a pouch of magic dust. She sprinkled it over herself, chanting the words of a spell:

Let me pass into the magic tree,
Where *fairy* unicorns *fly* wild and *free*.
Show me the trail of sparkling light,
To Unicorn Island, shining bright.

There was always a moment, especially when she'd been away for a while, when Zoe feared the magic would stop working. But soon came a faint tingling feeling, starting in her fingers and her toes, and she knew the spell had taken hold. With a *whoosh* she felt herself begin to shrink down, down, down, until the bushes in the garden were like mountains, towering above her.

"At last!" Zoe whispered to the night air. She ran between the roots of the oak tree, into the tunnel ahead, following the path of glimmering light. The floor was soft and sandy beneath her bare feet, and then, rounding a corner, she caught a glimpse of Unicorn Island.

It looked just as beautiful as ever. Zoe stepped out into the Silvery Glade, gazing at the fluttering leaves, in a riot of rainbow colours, and the glittering birds swooping through the clear blue sky.

With a grin, Zoe reached into her bag again, this time for a golden bell – her gift from the Unicorn King. She rang it three times, its musical chimes floating through the air.

It didn't take long before she heard beating hooves and Astra, her best friend on Unicorn Island, came galloping towards her. She would have recognized Astra anywhere, with her gleaming white coat, flecked with silver stars, and her horn, shining like an ocean pearl.

"Zoe!" Astra called. "You're back! I was with my mother in the glade when I heard your bell, and I came straight away..."

Zoe flung her arms around Astra's neck and breathed in the soft honey scent of her.

"Oh!" Astra went on. "I've been longing to see you again. I've got so much to tell you."

"What's happened?" asked Zoe. Hearing the excitement in Astra's voice, she decided

her own news could wait.

"Well..." Astra began. "I can hardly believe it, but the Unicorn King told me that he's so impressed by my magic, he thinks that one day I could be a Guardian like my mother!"

"A Guardian!" gasped Zoe. The Guardians were the most magical unicorns on the island, apart from the King. Astra's mother, Sorrel, was Guardian of the Trees, which meant she cared for all the trees and woodland creatures. Zoe had met the other Guardians too – of the Flowers, Clouds, Rivers, Spells and Snow.

"Becoming a Guardian has always been your dream," said Zoe, smiling at her.

"I know!" said Astra. "Even when I couldn't do any magic at all!"

"Would you be Guardian of the Trees, like your mother?" asked Zoe.

"I don't know," Astra replied, her brow creasing in thought. "We didn't talk about that. The King didn't say when it might happen either, but..." She paused for a moment, then looked up, her eyes brimming with a mixture of mischief and hope. "I went to the library in the Unicorn King's Castle, and looked in a book – *The Laws of Unicorn Island.* It said that to become a Guardian, you have to pass three tests."

"What kind of tests?" asked Zoe.

"I'll show you!" said Astra. "I'll use a writing spell..." And as she spoke she chanted a spell, conjuring up the page of the book so it shimmered in the air in front of them.

To become a Guardian, a unicorn must do three things to help the island, and in ways that display exceptional magic.

But these are tasks a unicorn must set for themselves – and each task can only be attempted once.

Be warned: fail one task, you fail them all.

"Now I just need to think of three tasks..." Astra went on. "I mean, I know it sounds tricky, and maybe I'll fail..."

"But you must try!" said Zoe. "I believe in you! Just think – you could be the youngest Guardian ever."

Caught up in Astra's excitement, she reached forward to give her another hug.

"I have some news too," Zoe added, in a more serious voice.

"Is it about Shadow?" asked Astra.

Zoe nodded.

"I thought it might be," sighed Astra. "I don't suppose he's had a change of heart, and has decided he's sorry for all the terrible things he's done?"

Zoe thought back to all the times Shadow had tried to take over Unicorn Island – by flooding it, freezing it, casting a spell to kill the trees... all so he could become king. It was only in the final battle, when all the Fairy Unicorns had joined together, that they'd been able to defeat Shadow once and for all. The King had shrunk Shadow down and trapped him in the cage of magical vines – and now it was Zoe's job to make sure he never came back to the island.

"I don't think Shadow's sorry at all," said Zoe. "But right now, I think all he cares about is being set free. Look," she went on, pulling Shadow's note from her bag. "He's asked me to give this to the Unicorn King. I don't know what it says... but I'm worried it means trouble."

"We'd better take this to the King at once," said Astra. "Climb on my back, Zoe, and we'll fly together!"

Chapter Two

Astra bent her legs and Zoe climbed on her back, the movement coming back to her as if she'd never been away. Zoe leant forwards, her fingers tangling in the soft, silky hair of Astra's mane.

"Are you ready?" asked Astra.

Zoe gave a smile. "I'm ready," she said.

The next moment, Astra began beating

her gossamer wings and they were flying above the treetops and into the airy blue. Zoe gave a whoop of delight. "There's nothing more magical than flying," she thought.

The warm spring breeze blew through her hair, birds soared by her side and below her lay Unicorn Island, in all its spring beauty.

They flew over Fairtree Forest and followed the shimmering trail of Moon River, as it wound its way across the island.

"Oh! I can see the castle now!" cried Zoe. For there, above the gushing waterfall, was the Unicorn King's Castle, carved into the rock face, almost hidden from view. Vines hung down its side, moss covered its roof and magic seemed to sparkle from its windows.

Astra swept over the waterfall, its spray brushing Zoe's cheeks, and landed on the little bridge by the entrance.

"Thank you!" said Zoe, swinging herself from Astra's back. "It felt wonderful to be flying again."

They smiled at each other, then Astra stepped forward and rang the bell pull by the gate.

At once, the gates swung open. They walked under a stone archway and into the castle courtyard. Zoe's face lit up to see

Fairy Unicorns, busily trotting this way and that, their shining wings glinting in the sunlight. Some were carrying herbs from the castle gardens, others were busy pulling carts filled with supplies, or were deep in conversation.

"Greetings," said a familiar voice, and Zoe turned to see the Unicorn King himself, coming towards them from the other side of the courtyard. At his side was Eirra, Guardian of the Snow, with his circlet of delicate snowflakes.

Zoe gave a quick intake of breath. Eirra's coat glittered like frost on a sunlit morning, and as for the King... She had forgotten quite how magical he was – larger than the other unicorns, with a shining mane and tail, and a sparkling crown.

"Astra," said the Unicorn King, nodding at her, his voice deep and sonorous. "And Zoe! Welcome back to Unicorn Island. It is lovely to have you with us again."

"Thank you," said Zoe, smiling up at him. "But I'm not sure I've brought good news." She reached into her bag and pulled out the note. "I've brought a message from Shadow."

"Then we should attend to this in private," said the Unicorn King. "Follow me," he added, including Astra and Eirra in his glance.

Together, they followed the King across the courtyard, up winding stone steps, and into a grand room, with high arched ceilings and windows laced with ivy. The light that flooded in was almost green, glistening through the leaves, patterning the polished marble floor.

"Now, let's see what Shadow has to say," said the King, his expression grim. He muttered a spell beneath his breath and the note fluttered from Zoe's hands like a paper bird, its message transformed into sparkling words in the air.

I am ready to reveal where
the GRIMOIRE is hidden...
It is in the Sea Dragon's Cave,
in the Kingdom Under the Sea.
If you promise to let me go free,
I will tell you the secret of
how to retrieve it.

"The Grimoire!" uttered Eirra, after reading the message aloud. "Just imagine if we could have it again..."

"The most magical book on the island," said Astra, her face lighting up.

Zoe nodded. She had not forgotten it. The Grimoire contained the most powerful spells known to the unicorns. Shadow had stolen it and used it against them, and the King had been looking for it ever since.

"We would be so much safer from Shadow, and from anyone trying to attack us, if we had the Grimoire once more," said Eirra.

"I know," replied the King, turning to look at his friend and advisor. "But don't you think this sounds like one of Shadow's traps? I agree we need to get the Grimoire back, but we cannot rely on Shadow to help us. Who's to say the Grimoire really is in the Sea Dragon's Cave? And even if it is, can we trust Shadow to tell us the secret to retrieving it? I don't think so..."

Eirra sighed and looked away in thought. "You're right, Your Majesty," he said, after a while. "After everything we've been through with Shadow, it's not worth the risk. But Your Majesty," he continued, a questioning look in his eyes, "if you had the Grimoire, would you let Shadow go free?"

"I would," the King replied. "In the heat of battle, I vowed Shadow could never return to Unicorn Island, but if I had the Grimoire in my possession, there would be nothing left to fear from him. He no longer has his powers."

"Now, Zoe," said the King. "It was right of you to bring me the message, but tell Shadow from me, we are not yet ready to trust him, or let him go free."

"I'll let him know," said Zoe. "Thank you, Your Majesty."

The King smiled at her then. "Don't worry about this anymore," he said. "I will keep thinking on it. In the meantime, enjoy your visit to Unicorn Island. I'm sure Astra will take good care of you."

With that, Astra and Zoe turned to go, back across the courtyard, out through the castle gates and onto the bridge that arched over the waterfall.

"Well," said Zoe, "I suppose that's the end of that little adventure. What shall we do now?"

But Astra didn't reply. She was staring into the distance, a strange expression in her eyes.

"Astra?" said Zoe, thinking her friend was being unusually quiet. "Oh no!" she went on. "I know that look. What are you planning?"

Astra smiled, and Zoe could see she had been thinking hard, working out exactly what to do...

"Isn't it obvious?" said Astra. "This is our chance! We should go and find the Grimoire ourselves!"

Chapter Three

Zoe looked around, to make sure no one was listening.

"Astra! We can't go and look for the Grimoire by ourselves!" she whispered. "It's so risky. What if it's a trap, just like the King suggested? And Shadow said there was a secret to getting it back. We don't even know what that secret is!"

"True..." Astra replied, undeterred. "But do you remember what we said after we helped to defeat Shadow? We vowed we'd make it our mission to track down the Grimoire. And now we have a lead."

Zoe could see that Astra was almost bursting with excitement. Her hooves were sparkling, her eyes were shining...

"This could be my first task to help me become a Guardian," Astra went on. "If we succeed, I will have tested my magic and helped the island."

"I'm still not sure..." said Zoe. "You're normally the cautious one, Astra. And the Sea Dragon's Cave doesn't exactly sound safe. I'm not sure I want to meet a sea dragon."

"It's not a *real* sea dragon," said Astra,

laughing. "It's only called that because of the way the rock is shaped – the entrance looks like a sleeping dragon."

"Have you been there before?" asked Zoe.

"Not exactly," admitted Astra. She caught Zoe's expression, seeming to sense her uncertainty. "I think I need to explain myself better," Astra went on, her tone more serious now. "While you were away, I realized something important. It's us being *together* that gives me confidence. Before you came along, I couldn't even *do* magic. Now my magic is always there, but it's our friendship that makes me feel as if I can really do something with it – *good* things. Don't you feel the same way?"

"I do," said Zoe, smiling back at her friend.

"And I've really missed our adventures..." Zoe took a deep breath. "Well, we've come this far together. I'm sure we can do this too."

"Really?" said Astra.

"Really," said Zoe.

Astra gave a little dance of excitement.

"Okay, here goes," said Zoe, swinging herself onto Astra's back. "Sea Dragon's Cave here we come!"

"Hooray!" cried Astra. She stretched out her wings, catching a gust of wind so they began soaring away from the castle. Looking back, Zoe saw the spray from the waterfall catching the sunlight, forming a misty rainbow behind them.

"But we'll need a plan first," warned Zoe. "We can't simply fly straight there."

"I've been thinking about that, too," said Astra. "Our first step is to find someone to help us. We can't ask the King or the Guardians. They'll only try to stop us if they find out what we're doing."

"There must be someone else..." said Zoe.

"I was wondering..." Astra went on. "What about Tio?"

"Tio?" said Zoe, doubtfully. Tio was the apprentice to the Guardian of the Spells. He'd helped them before, but Zoe knew that Tio *really* didn't like breaking the rules. "He'll never help us without the King's permission."

"Aha!" said Astra, and Zoe could tell that she was smiling. "But what's the one thing Tio loves more than rules?"

"Spell books," said Zoe, grinning.

"Exactly," agreed Astra. "Can you imagine how excited he'd be to find the Grimoire and read it himself? I'm sure we can persuade him. And I happen to know he's in the Flower Meadows today, collecting flowers for his spells."

"Let's go to him now!" said Zoe.

Astra beat her wings even faster than before, and soon they were heading towards Moon River, skimming its silvery surface. Beyond lay the Flower Meadows,

awash with wild flowers,

dancing with bees and butterflies.

"Any sign of Tio?" asked Astra, as she flew over the tops of the flowers.

"Yes!" said Zoe. "Over there, at the foot of the mountains. I think I see him!"

And there, peeking up among the wild flowers, was a scruffy little unicorn, with two saddlebags bursting full of spell books, his mane poking out in all directions.

"Tio!" Zoe called, waving to him.

Tio looked up and smiled as he spotted them, and in no time at all, Astra was gliding down to land gracefully by his side.

"Zoe!" said Tio, his face lighting up with pleasure. "It's so lovely to see you again. When did you get here?"

"I've not been here long," said Zoe. "It's great to be back though, and to see Unicorn Island looking as beautiful as ever."

"And for once there's no need for any wild adventures," said Tio. "No threats to worry about. No monsters to face. You can relax, swim in the river, laze in the sunshine..."

"Well, about that..." Astra interrupted gently.

"Oh no!" groaned Tio. "This isn't only a

little visit, is it? What dangerous things have you two got planned?"

"It isn't dangerous at all," said Astra, pleadingly. "We just need your help with a little visit to the Sea Dragon's Cave."

"The Sea Dragon's Cave?" spluttered Tio. "In the Northern Sea? You mean the deepest cave on Unicorn Island?"

Zoe looked over at Astra, who wouldn't quite meet her eye. "You didn't mention that part," whispered Zoe.

"Why, in the King's name, would you want to go there?" asked Tio.

"Well, that's the exciting part," said Zoe. "Shadow has told the Unicorn King that's where the Grimoire is hidden."

At the word 'Grimoire' Tio's ears pricked

up. "Really?" he asked. "At last we know where it is! I can't think of anything better than reading the Grimoire. All those wonderful, ancient spells. I could learn so much from it..."

He stopped and looked at them both suspiciously. "But why aren't the Unicorn King and the Guardians going?"

"They think it might be a trap," admitted Zoe. "Shadow said that if the King promised to release him, then he'd let the King know how to retrieve the Grimoire. I don't think the King trusts Shadow enough to ask him. And I don't think he wants to be bound by a promise to Shadow either."

"But," Astra went on, "if we found the Grimoire, then the King wouldn't be forced to free Shadow *and* we'd have the spell book. Don't you see? It's a brilliant plan."

"All I see," said Tio, "is danger. You know I much prefer eating cake and drinking tea in the Castle to fighting monsters – or visiting underwater caves," he added.

"I know, Tio," said Astra. "But this is the *Grimoire* we're talking about."

Tio's eyes took on a faraway look. "The Grimoire!" he murmured. "I have to admit," he said, "that does make a difference. I am *very* tempted..."

"So you'll come?" asked Zoe.

"Well," said Tio, his eyes still dreamy. "Maybe just this once... but *only* because it's the Grimoire." He began to look around. "Oh dearie me," he said. "I'd better pack up my things. I was just looking at a book about spells for sneezes. Now, where did I put it?"

Zoe and Astra exchanged glances while Tio fussed around, dropping as many items as he picked up. Pieces of paper kept catching the breeze and fluttering out from his saddlebags.

"Here, let me help," said Zoe, suppressing a smile as she swiftly picked up his things and packed them away in his saddlebags.

"And are these your glasses?" she asked, spotting a pair under a wild rose bush.

"Oh yes," said Tio. "They're new. Thank you! I wondered where they'd got to..."

Zoe popped them on for him. "Very smart," she said, smiling at him, making Tio blush a rosy pink beneath his coat.

"Ready?" asked Astra, once Zoe was on her back once more.

"As ready as I'll ever be," said Tio. "I don't know how I let you two persuade me..."

Astra began beating her wings, taking to the sky before Tio could change his mind.

They flew together, north along Moon River, heading out to the open sea.

"It shouldn't take us too long," said Tio. "I just hope we don't bump into any of the Guardians as we go..."

But the skies were empty, save for the birds and a few Flower Unicorns in the distance. Zoe couldn't help noticing that the further north they flew, the colder it became. When at last they crested the Towering Cliffs, she caught her first glimpse of the Northern Sea, the waves rising up, raging and crashing against the rocks.

They stopped on the rocky shore, taking shelter beside a large boulder, pounded round and smooth by the waves.

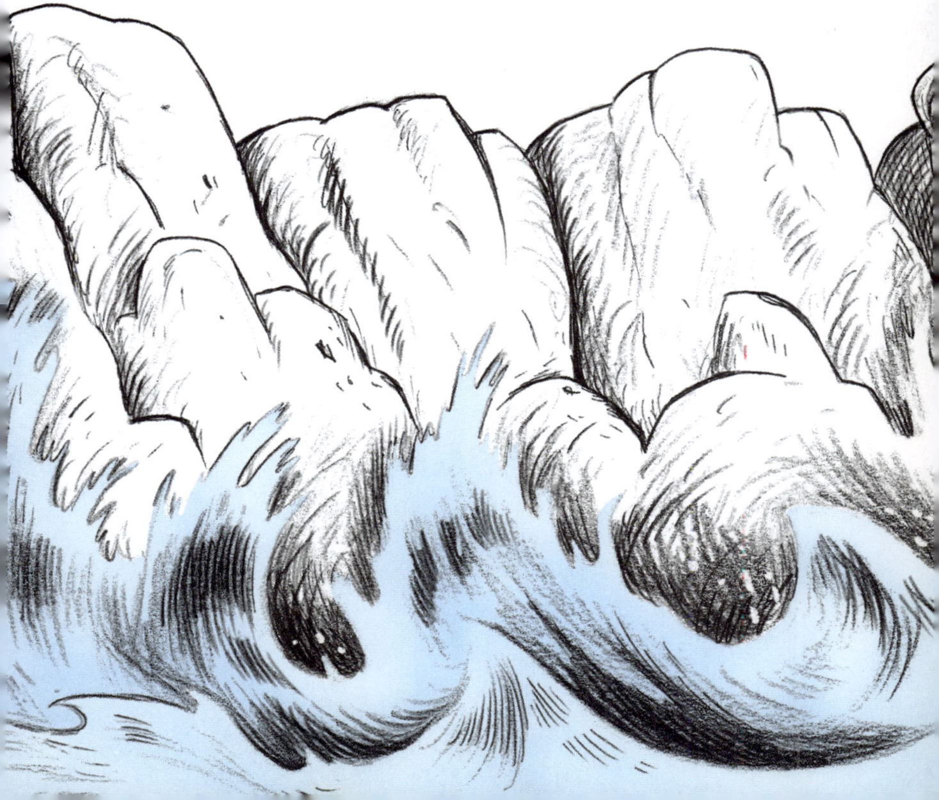

"How are we ever going to reach the cave?" asked Zoe. "The sea looks so stormy! Naida, the Guardian of the River, gave me some magic dust, so I can always enter Moon River, but will it work here?"

"Don't worry," said Tio. "I've got this!"

As he spoke, he pulled out a little pouch from his saddlebag. "This magic dust will let us breathe and talk underwater. It will protect my spell books, too! I just need to remember the spell for entering the Northern Sea..."

Zoe and Astra looked at him expectantly.

"Oh yes!" said Tio. "I know!"

He opened his mouth and then closed it again. "No, no, that one's for the Coral Sea," he muttered to himself. "Ah, here we are, the Western Sea!"

"Um... Tio," said Zoe, gently. "We need the spell for the *Northern* Sea."

"So we do," said Tio, beginning to nibble absent-mindedly on his pouch. He looked over at the pounding waves again, and Zoe could tell he was deep in concentration. Then his face lit up with a smile.

"Got it!" said Tio, suddenly.

And he began to chant, his voice taking on a deeper, more rhythmic tone, that made him appear suddenly older and more magical:

Oh Northern Sea, with waves so high
Reaching up to crest the sky,
From your raging, foaming spray
Make a tunnel, a magic way...

As he chanted the spell, it was as if the waves slowed and rose up to listen. Then they began to curl over at the top, creating a tunnel within the water.

"Wow!" said Zoe.

"That's amazing, Tio," gasped Zoe.

For a moment, Tio beamed with pride. Then he shook the pouch of magic dust, sprinkling it over them all.

"You go first, Astra," he said. "I'm always happier following."

Astra nodded at him. "Ready, Zoe?"

"Ready!" said Zoe, wrapping her arms around Astra, feeling the magic dust settle over her, the familiar tingling in her toes and fingers, and with it, a rush of anticipation. *Oh, how she'd missed this!*

"Then here goes!" said Astra, flying into the arching, swirling tunnel of water, Tio following close behind.

Chapter Four

They sped down the tunnel, deeper and deeper into the Northern Sea. Either side, Astra could see the shimmering shapes of the creatures that lived beneath the surface – jellyfish waving their tentacles, silver fish flashing their scales, long-armed octopuses

and gleaming sharks, their sleek bodies undulating like the waves.

At first, the light danced through the water in a kaleidoscope of colours, but the deeper they went, the darker it became.

"Do you know how much further it will be," asked Zoe, "before we reach the Sea Dragon's Cave?"

"Not long now," said Tio. "This tunnel leads all the way to the sea floor. Once we're there, the Sea Dragon's Cave should just be a short swim away."

"I'm so excited!" said Astra. "I've never been to the Kingdom Under the Sea before."

"The Kingdom Under the Sea?" said Zoe. "I didn't realize there was a whole kingdom beneath the waves?"

"Oh yes," Astra replied. "It's home to the Sea Unicorns. They're very secretive, mysterious creatures. They don't have legs like us, but sleek bodies that end in powerful tails, and long, thin, spiralling horns."

"They're proud too," added Tio, "always thinking that they're much better than us. They're led by a Queen, who is famous for her powerful sea magic."

"Oh!" said Zoe. "I'd love to meet them."

When the tunnel ended, and they swam out into the Underwater Kingdom, Astra and Tio each chanted a spell to light the way, their horns glowing like little torches.

"But where's the cave?" asked Zoe.

"Don't worry," said Tio, busy rummaging in his saddlebags. "I have just the thing... somewhere in here. Aha!" he cried, pulling out a map. "The Sea Dragon's Cave should be just beyond the next ridge."

The sea floor wasn't flat, as Zoe had imagined, but rose up and down, with little underwater hills and valleys. Zoe saw beautiful houses carved from coral and studded with mother-of-pearl. There were delicate archways, too, made of shells, and turrets that seemed to have no purpose other than to look beautiful. Zoe was awed by it, but everything seemed eerily abandoned, as if no one had been there for a long time.

“I wonder where all the Sea Unicorns are?” said Astra. “Shouldn’t they be here?”

“It is a bit odd...” said Tio, his brow creasing. “I have to say,” he added in a whisper, “I’m not sure I’m a big fan of this place. It’s a bit spooky, isn’t it?”

As they swam on, their voices grew

quieter, as if they were each weighed down by the silence all around them, and the sense of the vastness of the ocean.

Zoe tried to block out the flickering shadows at the edge of her vision, and the odd sense of being watched.

"Here we are," said Tio at last. "This must

be the Sea Dragon's Cave."

Ahead of them lay a huge cave. Curled around it, part of the rock face itself, was what looked like a giant sleeping dragon. The rock shone and sparkled, its dark surface flecked with silver.

"It's so life-like, isn't it?" whispered Astra.

"It really is," Zoe whispered back. "I can even see its scales. Do you think someone carved it? It can't be natural."

"I don't know," said Tio, backing away, "but whatever it is, I don't like it. I'm glad you're looking at its scales, because all I can see are those giant jaws..."

"Well don't look *there*, Tio," said Astra, coaxingly. "Just think of the Grimoire."

"Even the thought of the Grimoire isn't enough to make me go inside that cave," said Tio, with a shiver. "It's so dark down here... and menacing. I've helped you both get here, and that's enough. Besides, don't you think one of us should wait outside, and then if anything happens to you *inside* the cave, I can go and get help."

"So it's just us, then," said Zoe. She was standing beside Astra now, but she reached out to lay her hand against Astra's warm coat for reassurance. "I suppose there's no turning back..."

"No turning back," Astra repeated. And Zoe could tell she was trying to keep the fear from her voice. "We've come this far, Zoe. We can do this."

Then they began swimming towards the cave entrance.

"Just think," Astra said to Zoe, "the Grimoire could be just beyond the entrance. We could be so close."

But Zoe wasn't looking at the cave mouth. She was staring at the huge hunk of stone that looked like the dragon's head. "Um... Astra," said Zoe. "Are you sure the Sea Dragon is really sleeping?"

"What do you mean?" said Astra. "It's just a rock. Rocks can't sleep – or wake up."

"I think that's where you might be wrong," said Zoe. "I don't think it's a rock at all. I think it's a *real* dragon. And even worse... it's waking up!"

Astra followed Zoe's gaze. Sure enough,

one giant eyelid was slowly, slowly inching open. And there, looking straight back at them, was a huge, glinting eye.

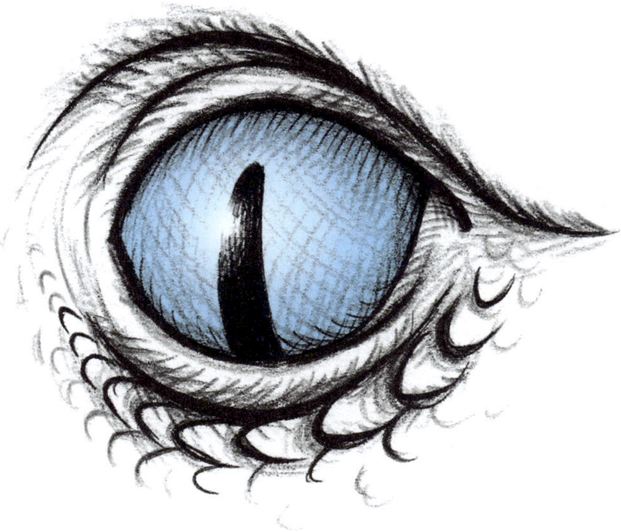

Chapter Five

Astra gave a gasp, her eyes fixed on the Sea Dragon, her body frozen to the spot. "Oh... my... goodness," she whispered. "It's definitely alive! Do you think it's seen us?"

"Yes," Zoe whispered back, trying not to make any movement. "I have a horrible feeling it's looking right at us."

"Now we know why the Sea Unicorns

don't live around here anymore," said Zoe, grimly. "They must have found out that the Sea Dragon can COME TO LIFE!"

Astra took a slow step backwards. "Let's try and move away. If we're very quiet, and very slow, maybe it won't notice us."

"Okay…" said Zoe, taking a step back, even though her legs felt like jelly.

"Tio…" Astra called out, as quietly as she could.

Tio's head popped up from behind a rock, a little distance away.

He took one look at the Sea Dragon, and gulped. "Oh crikey!"

The Sea Dragon was stirring, its giant head lifting away from the rock face. Its jaws began to gape open, revealing more of its long, dagger-like teeth.

"Tio, we're going to need help," said Astra. "Lots of help. I don't think the Sea Dragon has seen you yet. Please, swim as fast as you can. Find the Sea Unicorns and ask them to come and help."

"Too late!" said Tio, his voice quaking. "The dragon's looking right at me now. But I can cast a spell..."

He hurried back behind his rock, and began muttering a spell beneath his breath. Zoe could just catch his words, swirling away on the current...

...Come now, come quick,
Come *fast*, come soon.
Save us *from* our watery doom...

“Watery doom?” Zoe thought. “That really doesn’t sound good...”

By now the Sea Dragon was looming over them, a long, forked-tongue flicking

from its mouth. “How dare you wake me?” it hissed. “Did you think you could creep past me, and snatch the Grimoire while I slept?”

Zoe and Astra shook their heads, their eyes fixed on the dragon. Out the corner of her eye, Zoe could see Tio swim out from behind his rock and come over to join them.

“We stand together,” he said, as bravely as he could.

“Thank you, Tio,” said Zoe. “Sorry for getting you into this mess!”

“It was my choice,” said Tio. “Although I do think, in retrospect, it might have been a good idea *not* to come...”

“I wonder if Shadow planned this all along?” said Astra.

“I think Shadow’s more keen on being free than taking revenge,” said Zoe. “But Shadow’s the least of our worries right now.”

The Sea Dragon had inched closer, opening its jaws wider...

"Good point," said Astra, gazing up at the monstrous jaws.

"Do you think it's going to eat us?" said Tio, and Zoe could see that his knees had started to tremble.

"No," said Astra. "We're not going to let it. We have magic, too, remember. When it gets really close, we'll cast a spell to fight it off."

"Okay," gulped Tio. "It's just it's *really* big."

"I know," said Astra, keeping her voice even and calm. "Tio, did you cast that spell, calling for help?"

Tio nodded. "Doesn't seem like anyone's heard it yet, though. I suppose we are very, very deep down here, and very far away..."

But there was no more time for talking. At that moment, the Sea Dragon lunged forward and Astra began to cast a spell. Zoe could see the stars on her coat light up, just as they always did when her magic came to her, and sparks began to fizz from her horn.

"Come on, Tio," called Astra. "Join me. Use your magic!"

Together, Astra and Tio cast spell after spell, sparks flying from their gleaming horns, creating a protective bubble around the three of them.

"It's working!" said Zoe. "Look! The Sea Dragon can't reach us. Your spells are keeping it at bay. It keeps lunging but it can't get near us."

"We're not fighting it off though," said Tio,

sounding breathless now. "And I don't know how long we can keep going like this. The Sea Dragon's powers are different to ours – it has the magic of the sea – the magic that comes from the Underwater Kingdom. I'm not trained in it!"

Zoe looked to Astra. Her friend always seemed to have an answer, but Zoe couldn't see any hope in her eyes. "It's true," she said. "I don't understand its magic. Every time I try to cast a spell at it, the dragon swats it away. All my energy is going into stopping it from attacking us. How are we going to defeat it?"

"We'll find a way," said Zoe. She knew all she could do at this point was encourage her friends, to help them keep going… but then, looking around, she saw silvery shadows

gliding through the water towards them, glimmering in the darkness.

"Oh Tio!" she cried. "I think your call for help has been answered! I think I see them – the Unicorns of the Sea – and they're heading this way!"

They came swiftly through the dark

waters, leaving glittering trails in their wake. Zoe could see that the one at the front was the largest, with a glowing crown.

"We heard your call," said the Sea Unicorn, and even without the crown on her head, Zoe would have guessed she was the Queen. She sounded so commanding.

"So you've woken the Sea Dragon, have you?" she said, sternly. "We've always lived in fear that would happen again one day. The last time it came to life was long, long ago, and it took all the Sea Unicorns' powers to turn it back to stone. It's going to take all our magic, and more than a little luck, to make that happen again."

On those words, the Queen and her army of Sea Unicorns joined in the fight,

their spells crackling and sparking through the swirling current.

But though the dragon was kept at a distance, Zoe realized it was swatting away their spells, too. And she could see how quickly the Sea Unicorns were tiring. "Shadow said there was a secret to finding

the Grimoire," Zoe whispered to Astra. "I think he must have meant a secret to defeating the Sea Dragon."

"I agree," said Astra, grimly. "And from the looks of it, the Sea Unicorns don't know that secret any more than we do."

"I've got an idea," said Zoe. "While you're all keeping the Sea Dragon distracted, why don't I go into the cave and try to find the Grimoire?"

"You can't!" muttered Astra, between casting spells. "What if the Sea Dragon sees you and attacks?"

"I know it's a risk," said Zoe, determinedly. "But I'm sure I can sneak past it. I'm doing nothing, just standing here. And if something doesn't change soon, you're all going to be too tired to fight."

They locked eyes for a moment. "*Please*," said Zoe. "I must help."

"Okay," said Astra, taking a deep breath. "But be careful, Zoe."

Zoe gave a brief nod and began to swim

slowly, and as silently as she could, towards the cave entrance. She kept to the shadows, her eyes fixed on the Sea Dragon the whole time, to make sure it hadn't spotted her. But all its attention was focused on Astra, Tio and the Unicorns of the Sea, using its huge head and claws to swat away their spells, occasionally arching its scaly back to let them glance off its body.

The dragon's thrashing tail lay between her and the cave entrance. Zoe knew she was going to have to dart past it, and fast, hoping for the best. She waited a moment, summoning her courage, then swam hard, using all her strength. For a horrible moment, she saw the Sea Dragon's tail coming closer and closer towards her, but then with a final push, she was past it... and inside the cave.

No sooner had she swum beneath its arching roof, than she was plunged into darkness. "Oh no!" she thought. "How will I ever find the Grimoire in here? The cave could be huge and the spell book could be anywhere..."

Close to despair, Zoe began searching the cave floor with her hands – sweeping one way until she came to a wall, and then back the other way.

"What if the Grimoire is hidden?" she wondered. "Then I'll never find it in the darkness," she sobbed.

"Don't give up," she told herself, brushing away her tears. "Shadow didn't think we could get past the Sea Dragon, so he wouldn't have bothered *hiding* the Grimoire as well. I just have to search this cave thoroughly."

She kept working away, trying to keep track of where she was in the darkness, but with no idea of how large the cave might be, Zoe found it hard to stay hopeful. Then, as she raised her tired eyes, she saw a faint light shining through the water, somewhere deep at the back of the cave.

"Could that be it?" wondered Zoe. The Grimoire was said to hold the most powerful spells – perhaps it was so magical, it shone with a light of its own?

Zoe swam towards the light. It was terrifying, in the inky darkness, but the thought of Astra and Tio, battling the Sea Dragon, kept her going.

At last she reached the source of the light, and with a silent whoop of joy she saw that it really did come from the Grimoire. There was the ancient spell book, lying on the cave floor, its name inscribed in gold letters which shone through the

dark waters. And when Zoe reached down to pick it up, she realized a protective spell was keeping the pages safe from the water.

She hugged the Grimoire to her chest, then swam back towards the mouth of the cave, desperate now to get back to the others.

But when she reached the entrance, she found that the Sea Dragon's position had shifted. It was backed up against the mouth of the cave. Only a thin sliver was left between the Sea Dragon's body and the rock – too narrow for her to swim through.

"I'm trapped!" Zoe realized, her heart sinking. "This is the only way out! What am I going to do?"

Chapter Six

From inside the cave, Zoe could still hear the battle raging, and see the spells swirling in the current like underwater fireworks.

"We can't defeat the Sea Dragon!" cried one of the Sea Unicorns. "Nothing's working, even with all our spells combined."

At that moment, an idea struck Zoe. "What if the spell to defeat the Sea Dragon is *inside* the Grimoire," she thought. "Maybe that's what Shadow meant all along – he would know the spell to overcome the Sea Dragon because he's studied the Grimoire."

With trembling fingers, she began flicking through the pages of the book, desperately hoping to find the spell they needed.

And there it was... right in the middle of the book, in swirly silver lettering.

"But I don't have any magic," thought Zoe. "Nothing will happen if I say it... and what if the Sea Dragon hears me?"

She realized, though, this was their only hope. And so, she began to chant.

Just as Zoe had feared, the Sea Dragon turned at the sound of her voice, glaring at her with its angry eyes. Its jaws began to open, wider... and wider...

Zoe hastily retreated into the cave, shouting out the spell, her voice ringing out across the water.

Astra heard her first, and joined in the chant, followed by Tio, and then the Sea Unicorns all took up the spell, saying it over and over.

"It's working!" Zoe heard Astra cry. "Look! The tip of the dragon's tail is changing back to rock."

But now the dragon was beginning to lunge at her, white teeth gleaming, eyes flashing.

Zoe raised her arm to cover her face. She crouched down, shutting her eyes... and then she heard a loud shout. Astra, Tio and the Sea Unicorns were whooping and cheering and when Zoe opened her eyes she saw that the Sea Dragon had been turned to rock once more, just inches away from her.

Zoe raced out of the cave, still clutching the Grimoire, and Astra and Tio rushed to her side.

"Well done, Zoe," said Astra, beaming at her friend.

"You found it!" cried Tio, smiling. "At last we have the Grimoire!"

The Queen of the Sea Unicorns looked over at them. "I wouldn't be so sure about that," she said.

"What do you mean?" asked Astra.

"Hand over the Grimoire," said the Queen. "It belongs to *us* now. After all, it's in our realm. We can't let you just swim away with it. That book is far too powerful and precious for you."

"We know it's precious," said Tio, puffing himself up proudly. "That's why we came all this way to get it. And we're going to return it to its rightful owner... the Unicorn King!"

"And what's more," added Astra, "we thought you were on *our* side."

"There are no sides here," replied the Queen, calmly. "Of course we couldn't leave you to battle the Sea Dragon alone. But now we know the Grimoire is in our kingdom, we will do everything in our power to keep it. That book could help us more than you can imagine."

She eyed it, almost greedily, and Zoe clutched it all the tighter.

"There are more of them than us," Tio whispered. "And I'm exhausted! I really don't fancy fighting them all for it."

Astra looked over at the Queen, her eyes narrowed in thought. "How about a spell duel?" she suggested. "Just you and me. And the winner takes the Grimoire."

The Queen of the Sea Unicorns smiled. "Challenge accepted," she said.

"Um... just give us a moment," said Tio, holding up his hoof. Then he hurried Astra and Zoe out of earshot. "Astra!" he said. "You saw the Queen fight against the Sea Dragon. She's almost as powerful as the Unicorn King. If you do lose the spell duel, we'll have lost the Grimoire all over again."

"How does a spell duel work?" asked Zoe.

"We each cast a spell shape," Astra explained, "then wait to see which spell wins."

Zoe looked at Astra, who looked back at

her, unblinking. At once Zoe understood how sure Astra felt about this. Zoe nodded at her, an unspoken message passing between them.

"I trust Astra on this," said Zoe, turning to Tio. "Let her do the spell duel."

Tio rolled his eyes. "Fine," he said. "I just really hope this works!"

Astra stepped forward, calling out to the Queen. "Let's begin," she said.

They both bowed their heads, and began muttering their spell. As she listened, Zoe realized that the Queen's spell was in another language, but it seemed to her to speak of water and tides and crashing waves. Then all around the Queen, swirling in glittering blue, a whirlpool appeared, spiralling out from her horn. To Zoe, it showed the strength of the sea, the beauty and danger of their kingdom, and how much the Sea Unicorns needed the Grimoire.

Then she turned to look at Astra, and saw that her spell was all about Unicorn Island. She was conjuring up images of the Flower Meadows, Moon River, the Castle and, last of all, the Silvery Glade, where she lived with her mother. Zoe could see Astra was showing everything she loved about Unicorn Island, everything she held precious and wanted to protect. The pictures burst out from her horn in dazzling, rainbow colours.

"It's beautiful!" gasped Zoe.

"But it's not strong enough," Tio whispered to her. "Look! The Queen's spell is winning."

And Zoe could only watch in dismay as

the Queen's great whirlpool began to suck in Astra's glittering tapestry of Unicorn Island... until all that was left of Astra's spell was an oak tree.

"It's the Great Oak!" Zoe realized – the tree that connected Astra's world to hers.

But at the very last moment, the branches of the oak tree began to spread out. They took hold of the whirlpool and spun it around... then the tree seemed to swallow it whole, its trunk widening as the whirlpool disappeared inside.

"You did it, Astra!" cried Tio.

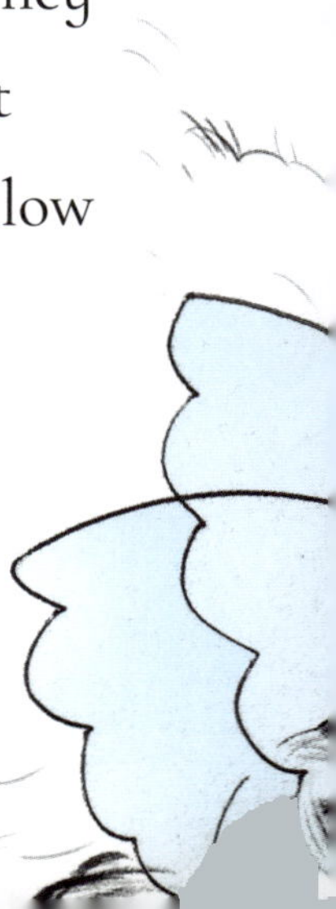

The Queen bowed her head. "You have won the duel. The Grimoire is yours to keep. I can see how much you love your home and that this precious book will be safe with you."

"Thank you," said Astra.

Then the Sea Unicorns turned away, slipping back through the water, leaving behind only their ghostly, silvery trails.

"Well done, Astra," said Zoe, hugging her. "I always knew you could do it."

"Oh, me too," said Tio, with a grin, as Zoe tucked the Grimoire safely into his saddlebag. "Now, I don't know about you two, but I've had enough excitement for one day. I think it's time to go home."

Chapter Seven

Astra, Tio and Zoe made the journey back in silence, each exhausted by the epic events of the day. By the time they reached the Unicorn King's Castle, they were also feeling more than a little nervous.

"I've been thinking," said Tio, as Astra went to pull the bell rope. "The King might not be that happy with us. After all, it was a bit risky, going to find the Grimoire ourselves."

"Do you think we're going to be told off?" asked Zoe.

Astra nodded. "We're definitely going to be told off. But we've brought back the Grimoire, remember? The most precious spell book on the island. So we can't be in *that* much trouble."

Tio gulped. "Well, here goes," he said, as Astra rang the bell.

The gates swung open and, taking a deep breath, Astra and Tio trotted through to the castle courtyard, Zoe following close behind.

"Uh oh," whispered Astra, for standing before them wasn't just the King, but each and every one of the Guardians, including Astra's mother, Sorrel.

"Zoe!" said Sorrel. "Welcome back to Unicorn Island. The King told me you were here and I was hoping to see you."

Zoe smiled back at Sorrel, and then turned to the King, knowing the moment had come to tell everyone what they'd done.

"We've got something for you, Your Majesty," she said. And, without another word, she reached into Tio's saddlebag and handed him the Grimoire.

Everyone gasped. "Is that... is that really the Grimoire?" asked Lily, Guardian of the Flowers.

"It is!" said Medwen, Guardian of the Spells, leaning forward to take a closer look.

Sorrel frowned. "But the King was just telling us that the Grimoire was in the Sea Dragon's cave. You can't possibly have found it there. It's one of the deepest caves in the Northern Sea."

"And what's more," said the King, looking stern, "you heard me say that we wouldn't be going there in case it was a trap."

"And was it?" asked Eirra, Guardian of the Snow.

"I think we'd better tell you the whole story," said Astra. "But please remember – we only wanted to help."

And so she began to tell them what had happened – from Tio's spell to help them through the stormy Northern Sea, all the way to the Sea Dragon's Cave. She described how the Sea Dragon woke, and how they'd tried to fight it, until the Sea Unicorns came to their aid, and how brave Zoe was, swimming into the cave to find the Grimoire.

Then Tio took over the telling, explaining

about the spell duel and how Astra defeated the Queen of the Sea Unicorns.

And all the time, Zoe anxiously watched their expressions. Sorrel, she could see, had turned pale with shock, while Eirra looked on sternly. The Unicorn King's face was inscrutable.

When Tio had finished, everyone stood silent for a moment. Then, clearing his throat, the King stepped forward.

"I think you all knew what you were doing was wrong, or you would have told us where you were going and what you were up to. If any of you had come to harm, none of this would have been worth it."

He turned and looked at Astra. "In the past," he said, "you've been a cautious unicorn, always thinking things through. That is how a leader should be. I gathered the Guardians around me today to decide what to do, but you jumped ahead with your plan, putting Zoe and Tio in danger. Why did you do it? Was it your wish to become a Guardian? Because simply fulfilling the three tasks alone won't achieve that. I also have to decide that you're ready and after today..."

Astra hung her head in shame. "I'm sorry. I was so excited about the thought of becoming a Guardian, and the strength of my new-found magic… I got carried away. I can see that now."

"Are you truly sorry?" asked the King.

"I am," said Astra, nodding in reply. "When the Sea Dragon woke and I realized its magic was different to ours… I was so worried about what would happen… I knew I'd put everyone in danger. We came so close to losing the Grimoire too – I couldn't have borne it if we'd lost it to the Sea Unicorns, and all because of me."

"I'm sorry too," added Tio. "I was so excited by the thought of reading the Grimoire. I never should have gone along with the plan."

"Well," said the King, "you have all learned an important lesson today." Then, at last, his face broke into a smile. "And I cannot deny it," he went on. "Today, the three of you have helped make Unicorn Island a safer place. We finally have our most magic book back in our land. I cannot regret what you've done. Though you should never have set out on this dangerous mission, you all acted with great courage."

Zoe, Astra and Tio couldn't help exchanging smiles.

"I think this calls for a feast," said Nimbus, Guardian of the Clouds. "I always think that's the best way to celebrate."

"I agree," said Medwen, Guardian of the Spells. "And I know exactly which spell to cast! May I?" he said to the King.

"Of course," the King replied.

Medwen went over to the Grimoire blowing the pages until he came to the chapter he wanted – 'Spells for Delicious and Sumptuous Feasts'.

"You see," said Medwen, turning to Astra, Tio and Zoe, "the Grimoire doesn't just have powerful spells for saving the island. It also has an excellent section on feasting!"

And with that, he began to chant a spell...

Conjure a *feast* that is *fit for* a dream,
With bubbling peach juice
and raspberry pie.
Chocolates and cookies,
marshmallows and cream,
And pro*f*iterole towers,
right up to the sky...

Zoe watched in amazement as the words of his spell became real. The courtyard was transformed into a delectable picnic. There were tables laden with food, bunting

fluttered in the breeze and baubles hung jauntily from the trees.

"This is incredible!" gasped Zoe.

"I never think a feast is complete without some music," said the Unicorn King. And he conjured a spell of his own, until the most beautiful music was wafting through the air.

"Now let's feast!" said the King.

But Zoe and Astra hung back, seeing Sorrel coming over towards them.

"I'm almost glad I didn't know what you two were up to today," she said. "I would have been so worried. I don't ever want you to put yourselves in danger like that again... but I'm also hugely proud of you both. And Astra," she went on, "to have won a Spell Duel against the Queen of the Sea Unicorns is an amazing feat."

"I couldn't have done it without Zoe and Tio," said Astra.

Zoe grinned back at her. "We make a great team," she said.

"You do," said the King, coming up to them. "And it was very brave of you to go into the cave to get the Grimoire, Zoe. We're so grateful to have it back."

After that, Zoe and Astra joined the feast until the sun began to slip down the sky, lighting it with a fiery orange glow.

"Time for you to go home, Zoe," said Sorrel. "Astra will see you back to the Great Oak. But please, come again soon."

"Thank you," said Zoe. "I will. I promise."

"And next time," said the Unicorn King, "bring Shadow with you. Now we have the Grimoire, we can finally set him free. We have nothing to fear from him anymore."

"But then Shadow has got what he wanted!" said Tio.

"Not exactly," said the King. "Shadow didn't force us to release him. You three managed to retrieve the Grimoire without any help from him. We're letting him go because it's the right thing to do. And he'll still be without his powers, and the ability to do harm."

Zoe nodded, then turned to Tio. "Goodbye," she said. "It was wonderful to go on another adventure with you."

Tio laughed. "I don't know how a unicorn like me ends up on your madcap adventures. It's not my thing at all. But from now on, I will very happily be spending my time studying the Grimoire!"

With a final wave to all her unicorn friends, Zoe swung herself up onto Astra's back. Together, they cantered through the castle gates, then Astra spread her wings wide and took to the skies.

"To think," said Zoe, as they flew, "that I thought I was going to have a relaxing time today! Instead, we've battled a Sea Dragon, I've chanted a spell from the Grimoire and

you've fought a Spell Duel."

"And don't forget the feast!"

"How could I?" laughed Zoe, clutching her tummy. "I'll never be hungry again!"

They soared over the island, until, as the last light began to fade, Astra touched down in the Silvery Glade, just by the entrance to the Great Oak.

Zoe slid from Astra's back and gave her friend one last hug.

"Goodbye," she said, turning towards the tunnel that led back to her world. "I'll come again – as soon as I can. And maybe next time, we can work out a way to bring you one step closer to becoming a Guardian."

Astra smiled. "I couldn't do any of this without you, Zoe. Thank you!"

Zoe gave a final wave and started running back along the secret tunnel. "Another wonderful adventure on Unicorn Island," she thought. "And I can't wait for my next one..."

Edited by Lesley Sims
Designed by Brenda Cole
Reading consultant: Alison Kelly

First published in 2022 by Usborne Publishing Ltd., Usborne House,
83-85 Saffron Hill, London EC1N 8RT, England. usborne.com